Faith in the Midst...
STUDY GUIDE

A Companion
Bible Study
to
THE ROSE GARDEN
AND THE RING

Lynn and Christine

WESTBOW
PRESS®
A DIVISION OF THOMAS NELSON
& ZONDERVAN

Scripture taken from the Holy Bible, NEW INTERNATIONAL VERSION®. Copyright © 1973, 1978, 1984, 2011 by Biblica, Inc. All rights reserved worldwide. Used by permission. NEW INTERNATIONAL VERSION® and NIV® are registered trademarks of Biblica, Inc. Use of either trademark for the offering of goods or services requires the prior written consent of Biblica US, Inc.

Scripture quotations taken from the Holy Bible, New Living Translation, Copyright © 1996, 2004. Used by permission of Tyndale House Publishers, Inc., Wheaton, Illinois 60189. All rights reserved.

Scripture is taken from GOD'S WORD®, © 1995 God's Word to the Nations. Used by permission of Baker Publishing Group.

Scripture taken from the New Century Version. Copyright © 2005 by Thomas Nelson, Inc. Used by permission. All rights reserved.

WestBow Press books may be ordered through booksellers or by contacting:

WestBow Press
A Division of Thomas Nelson & Zondervan
1663 Liberty Drive
Bloomington, IN 47403
www.westbowpress.com
1 (866) 928-1240

ISBN: 978-1-5127-2749-4 (sc)
ISBN: 978-1-5127-2750-0 (e)

Library of Congress Control Number: 2016901054

Print information available on the last page.

WestBow Press rev. date: 2/26/2016

Dedication

This bible study is dedicated to all those people who are Christian but are lost and confused about what is happening in their life. It is for those who want to understand more of what they are going though and how *they* feel about the issues. Besides ourselves, we have many dear friends who continually struggle with what has happened in their life. Our hope is that when they complete this bible study, they can forge into their future knowing where they are now and which direction they are going…always knowing they are not alone. Realizing where the Lord is in the midst of their everyday life and how He will walk right alongside of them is our sincerest prayer!

In Christ's Love,
Lynn and Christine

Contents

Introduction

Welcome! After two years of hard work, long hours, many prayers, several boxes of tissues and supporting one another throughout it all, our story, *The Rose Garden and the Ring*, was completed. A few dear friends blessed us by reading through the book and giving us their thoughts. The suggestion was made that a bible study would make a good companion to the book, helping others get through the same thing. We began to pray over the advice and received confirmation that a bible study guide would be our next adventure!

Although this bible study was written as a companion to the original book, *it can certainly stand alone!* It can be used as a six week, four day a week study for a group or for an individual. If used as a group study, we encourage you and your study leader to determine the needs of the group and proceed accordingly. Our choice was to use the NIV version of the Bible for the majority of the fill in the blanks and other sections; any deviation from that would be noted in the text.

We are by no means bible scholars but are faithful servants who have been called to encourage others. Every step of this study has been lovingly penned with prayer first and then words. We are so glad you will be joining us for a time of learning, self-awareness, and healing. As this study was being written, we were deeply involved in our own struggles. We wrote from a view point of current and past pain, working through our issues all along the way. It is real, it is raw and it is a discovery of self and faith. Our hope is that you will be able to obtain a better understanding of what you are going through and how to proceed through faith as well!

AS A GROUP STUDY...

Your bible study is most likely comprised of a group of people facing multiple life issues…not just adultery. However, if you feel like adultery is the predominate issue in your gathering; our suggestion would be to use the book as a read along through the chapters. The chapters from *The Rose Garden and the Ring* coincide with the chapters' number in the study guide. The study guide is set up with six week themed parts of four day sections in each week.

AS AN INDIVIDUAL STUDY...

Wake up, go to work, come home, make dinner, clean up, go to sleep, and start over the next day. We are continuously keeping ourselves so busy with whatever we can to avoid thinking about what causes us heartache, putting "self" on a back burner. Your individual reason for needing healing, we cannot predict. The outcome we hope for is wholeness in your heart and in faith. Take time as you go through this guide to let God in and get real! You deserve to live a better life, complete with healing and Christ centeredness. Problems don't get fixed overnight, or even with one study guide. The work you put in will assist in releasing the healing power of the Lord in your life. That is our ultimate desire for you!

ACTION ITEMS: As you gather each week, begin by discussing the previous week's actions in addition to some of the material found in the four lessons per week. Be sure to encourage completion of each action at the end of the discussion as this will enrich their experience.

Let us pray for you…

Heavenly Father, as the two of us humbly come before you, we ask that those who need to hear these words are drawn to this study. We know there are no accidents, only divine appointments. As they open themselves up to hear your word, help them to walk with you and grow in faith. We understand time is precious so we fervently ask you help show each person opportunities for this study to be completed sometime during their day. We seek healing and refuge from our current storms; you are our strong tower! Our faith, hope and trust are in you.

Amen

Week 1

Begin with the Basics

Day 1, Chapter 1

How 'Big' is Your Faith?

"Now faith is confidence in what we hope for and assurance about what we do not see." (Hebrews 11:1)

What is happening? What am I supposed to do? This doesn't seem real. How could you let this happen to me? No matter what you are currently facing or what has happened, God is there. You have to make an important decision. Are you going to follow God in the path He has chosen for you or are you going to do what the world says for you to do and choose your own path? When faced with these two options, what is your decision?

I am overwhelmed...
- Read Psalm 18:4-5____
- Now read Psalm 18: 6 and fill in the blanks.

> "In my _____ I _____ to the Lord; I _____ to my
> God for _____. From his temple he _____;
> my cry came before him, into his_____."

Question: What specific hurdles are you finding hard to jump over at this time?
(i.e.: getting up in the morning, seeing a future, what do I do now/which way to turn)

Question: How can you approach each hurdle with God by your side?

Maybe for you not everything appears to be what it seems. The truth is not the truth, your life is taking a drastic turn from where you thought you were headed, and you have no clue where to begin. Call to the Lord, tell him everything you are thinking and feeling. He can help you sort out the details.

I am confused...
- Read Deuteronomy 4:35

Question: What is the most important concept for you to grasp in this scripture?

_____

_____

_____

- Read Deuteronomy 7:9

Question: What are the two concepts to take from knowing God is God?

_____

_____

_____

I am hurt and need comfort...

Question: What hurts you the most about your situation? Share the top two (or 50 ☺).

_____

_____

_____

_____

_____

- Where do you find hope in God's promises? Read Psalm 119:49-52 and check all that apply.
    - ☐ Your family
    - ☐ God's Word
    - ☐ Tabloids
    - ☐ God's Law
    - ☐ Clean laundry

In our desperation we search many places for answers. But the true answers are in God's word, His promises, and His law.

I am angry...

You might have been betrayed. You may have lost a loved one. You don't know who you are anymore. You don't know who your spouse or your friends are anymore. You have been planning a future and living day to day towards a future that included you both and any children in it. Of course you are angry and it is okay to be mad but...

- Read James 1:20 and fill in the blanks.

"Human _____ does not produce the _____ that God desires."
Instead...

- Read Ephesians 4:26

Question: What does God tell us NOT to do in the above scripture?

_____

_____

_____

Whatever the situation, your anger needs to be transformed.

I need guidance...

"Your word is a lamp to my feet and a light for my path. I have taken an oath and confirmed it, that I will follow your righteous laws." (Psalm 119:105)

A lamp and a light are the same thing right? Why did this verse mention both? A lamp shines right in front of your feet; it shows each step you should take. A light illuminates what lies ahead. Pray for guidance on what path you should take and follow it. God is there with you every step of the way.

Action: Call out to God. You can tell Him anything. Know that the Lord is faithful. Choose to listen and learn God's word.

Day 2, Chapter 2

Walking with God

"Your own ears will hear him. Right behind you
a voice will say, 'This is the way you should go,'
whether to the right or to the left." (Isaiah 30:21)

In chapter 1, How 'Big' is Your Faith?, we learned to choose to walk with God wherever that leads us rather than follow where the world thinks we should go. But what does that mean? How do we do that?

Picture a young child walking with her father. As a little one, she believes that her daddy has her best interest at heart and is there to protect, lead, and guide her. He reaches out and asks her to hold his hand. She happily takes his hand and they cross the street safely, without a doubt that they will reach the other side. The Lord wants to lead us safely through our trials. He is reaching out his hand, all we need to do is take it, trust, and walk with Him.

Question: How have you experienced God walking you through your pain?

_____

_____

_____

Question: Has there been a situation in which you chose not to not take His hand and cross the street alone? How did that work out for you?

_____

_____

_____

_____

_____

- Read 1Thessalonians 1:4-6 and fill in the blanks.

*"Paul, Silas, and Timothy say to the church of the Thessalonians,
"For we know, brothers and sisters loved by God, that he
has _____, because our gospel came to you not simply
with _____ but also with _____, with the _____ and
deep conviction. You know how we lived among you for your sake.
You became imitators of us and of the Lord, for you welcomed
the message in the midst of _____
with the _____."*

Question: To you, who or what is the Holy Spirit and what role does "He" play in your life?

_____

_____

_____

*"But the advocate, the Holy Spirit, whom the Father will
send in my name, will teach you all things and will remind
you of everything I have said to you." (John 14:26)*

The Holy Spirit is here to teach, sometimes convict, but also to remind us of the joy that we can have through Christ. We pray that you can learn to hear the gentle voice of the Holy Spirit and encourage you to study more about its purpose in your life on your own.

**Action: The Lord wants to lead us safely through
our trials. LET HIM! Ask God through the Holy
Spirit to teach and guide you every day.**

Day 3, Chapter 3

Immediate Assistance/Guidance

"Submit yourselves, then, to God. Resist the
devil, and he will flee from you." (James 4:7)

It would be amazing to have access to a 911 number directly linking callers to an angel who would in turn put us on a very short, praise music filled hold, until returning with God's answer for our emergency. It is fun to think about but obviously not realistic. We need his guidance when in trouble, but how do we get it?

Question: Especially in today's world, how do you trust fully in God?
* What does it mean to trust? Write your own definition of the word.

_____

_____

_____

The dictionary defines trust as "reliance on the integrity, strength, ability, surety, etc., of a person or thing; confidence." (Dictionary.com, 2015) The Word says, "Trust in the Lord with all your heart." (Proverbs 3:5). Do you rely on God's integrity, strength, and ability to see you through your daily struggles? Check one answer below.
   ❑   YES!
   ❑   NO ☹
   ❑   NOT REALLY
   ❑   WHATEVER SHE SAYS

* Define in your own words "to control"

_____

_____

_____

The dictionary defines "to control" as "to exercise restraint or direction over; dominate; command." (Dictionary.com, 2015) The

Word says, "...in all your ways submit to him, and he will make your paths straight." (Proverbs 3:6) The Lord doesn't sit on you or control you like a robot. He does, however, help you to show restraint or guide your steps.

- Now consider the word "submit." How does the word "submit" make you feel?

  _____

  _____

  _____

One of the definitions of the word "submit" is to give power and authority to someone else. Another definition is "to present for approval, consideration, or decision of another." (Dictionary.com, 2015) It is not that we cannot have ideas and thoughts of our own, but it is that we are able to "submit" those ideas to God for approval. Consider the following...

Example 1: A 19 year old boy living at home does not need permission from his parent to go to the movies but telling his parent what his plans are is being respectful to the parent and acknowledges that the parent is still the head of the household.

Example 2: A child is having trouble with a friend at school and tells the parent about it. The child does not necessarily want the parent to fix the issue for them but rather guide them. In the same way, pray to God with your struggles, ask for guidance and trust in His response. After all, He is our heavenly father.

- Read Mark 9:14-29.

Question: How can we overcome our non-belief?

_____

_____

_____

- Read Proverbs 3:5-6 and fill in the blanks.

> "_____ in the Lord with all your heart
> and_____; in all your ways
> submit to him, and he will make your _____."

What is happening all around you does not have to make sense and probably will not anyway. Your emotions are all over the place especially in the beginning of a trial. Do not depend on your own personal interpretation of what is going on, simply trust that God knows and hears.

Action: Rely on God's strength, integrity and ability. Present your plans and thoughts to God for approval whether in writing and prayer or simply with prayer. Your answer may not make sense, but God is in control, and He sees the bigger picture.

Day 4, Chapter 4

Tools and Weapons

"He gives strength to the weary and increases
the power of the weak." (Isaiah 40:29)

In your weakness you can find strength when you walk with Jesus. Let's face it…this is a fight. You are fighting yourself, you are fighting the person who wronged you, and you are sometimes even arguing with God. You will be responding to your situation in many ways.

Question: What are some of the emotions you personally are fighting? Are you fighting with yourself or with someone else?

•   Read 2 Corinthians 10:4-5

"The weapons we fight with are not the weapons of the world. On the contrary, they have divine power to demolish strongholds. We demolish arguments and every pretension that sets itself up against the knowledge of God, and we take captive every thought to make it obedient to Christ."

A stronghold can be positive or negative. It can be a fortress of walls built up in our minds to keep us safe from harm. Surrounding yourself with God's word is a good stronghold. Putting up walls with your spouse is a bad stronghold. What are those walls in each scenario made from? Are they truth and strength or bitterness, resentment, and pride?

Question: What are some of your strongholds? What are those "walls" made of?

....

....

....

Question: How can you break down the harmful walls?

....

....

....

Taking every thought captive is the first step in making a dent in your wall. When we take our thoughts captive we are identifying our personal barriers and focusing on tearing down those barriers one brick at a time. You need a weapon to demolish a wall. Some of God's weapons are: His word, which is our guide; prayer, our communication with Him; the Holy Spirit, who is our intercessor; our faith, that God is omnipresent; our hope, that God will lead us through this; and love, God's unconditional love for us. The world offers weapons that may be useful, such as counselors and the support of friends, but, be careful, they may not necessarily have the backing of divine power.

- List the six weapons mentioned in the preceding paragraph.
  1. ....
  2. ....
  3. ....
  4. ....
  5. ....
  6. _____

So...let's just say that you have decided to use a few of God's divine weapons to break down your walls. Where does that leave you when they are down? Most likely you will feel vulnerable and unprotected against another emotional attack. Thus, more than not, people choose to keep their walls up to avoid pain. This is where we need to make a choice. Will I give this issue to God or keep it? What decision will you make?

EXTRA: Read Ephesians 6:10-18 (Armor of God)

God's armor should be put on daily. Find your perfect time whether first thing in the morning or before bed to commit to the Lord.

Action: Make YOUR choice. Choose to give your situation to God or kept it. Then...Own it!

Week 2

Am I Going Crazy?

Day 1, Chapter 5

Loss of Control/Power

"Cast all your anxiety on him because
he cares for you." (1 Peter 5:7)

True story #1:

After facing numerous betrayals, one woman had enough of being hurt. The Holy Spirit and multiple prophetic words had instructed her to stay in the marriage. She was a strong woman who had relied on God each time her husband had returned to the marriage. She worked on forgiveness and healing. She worked on her friendship with her husband, scheduled date nights and tried to forget. She worked on bringing the family "back to normal". But she had one secret she held in her heart, her wall. Probably, it wasn't really that much of a secret. Those who knew her could see it, and God could really see it. Her secret was that she decided not to love, or at least not in a romantic way.

The secret was her stronghold. Not saying "I love you" was her protection against future pain. If she said it, her wall would crumble, and so would she. What was she to do? She was choosing to continuously hurt herself and her spouse by holding up the wall. She loved the Lord and her children, but, in her opinion, it was not an option for her spouse to receive her love any more. What do you think she should do?

The Word says she should use his divine weapons (Chapter 4) to remove the walls, but that leads to the problem of vulnerability. The only option for her is to trust in His care for her. Nahum 1:7 says *The Lord is good, a refuge in times of trouble. He cares for those who trust in Him"*. That is where she can place her faith and hope. God's ultimate and unconditional love for the strong woman will assure her a safety the walls cannot provide!

True Story #2:

Another woman's husband started drinking to excess, causing extreme physical and emotional pain to her and the children in multiple ways. He became a full alcoholic and lost his job. She continued to go to church and gave the situation to God, time after time, but then would take matters into her own hands again and again and again. The situation continued to go downhill. She was faced with short-selling the home herself. After unsuccessfully trying to save the marriage she also faced divorce.

At what seemed like all at the same time, she had an alcoholic husband, faced divorce, lost a home, became a single mother, struggled with children who were bitter and angry, and to top it all off, found out that she had stage three breast cancer. What was this woman to do now? The choice was really easy for her to make at this point. She couldn't handle everything so she gave it *all* to the Lord. As you can imagine, she was so overwhelmed she didn't want to take any of it back to solve on her own! Her trust was solely in the Lord and His provision for a way out. Thankfully, he did in time. She found a new home, amicably divorced, recovered from cancer, finished her master's degree, attended many years of counseling with the kids, got a job, and trusted in the Lord through the entire process. Obviously, this was a very long and difficult journey. Life isn't perfect or easy for her now but there is no doubt the Lord kept his promises and continues to care for her.

Most of us give an issue over to the Lord, take it back, give it, and take it, and so on until we finally come to a point of true release to our capable Father!

Question: In what area or areas in your life have you recently struggled with loss of control or power?

Whether your difficulties are financial, health related, the children, your marriage, or any other of the many burdens we carry, there is only one way to regain that sense of control. You must get to the point of completely losing control to gain it again. The Lord is waiting to gently take it from your hands and carry it for you. Just *choose* to ask!

Question: What is at least one area of your life you can *choose* to give to God right now?

Truth

This word can elicit a flood of thoughts and emotions when one is dealing with betrayal or loss.

Question: Off the top of your head, what is your definition of the word "truth"?

Does your definition reflect the human view of truth or God's view of truth? Those who are hurting need to focus on His truth, because human "truths" fail us time and time again. No matter what your definition of truth is, God's truth is unfailing and unchanging.

John 17:17 says, *"Sanctify them by the truth; your word is truth."* It is right there. The bible says that His word is the truth. Therefore, we simply need to look in the scripture to find the truths we seek. You may not like what you find because it might require you to be humble, forgiving, loving, or any other emotion or action that seems undeserving but deep down you know that God is right.

- Redefine "truth" from God's perspective.

Action: Pray this scripture daily: "Teach me to do your will for you are my God. May your gracious spirit lead me forward on a firm footing." (Psalm 143:10 NLT)

Day 2, Chapter 6

Emotions...the Rollercoaster

"In my anguish I cried to the Lord, and he
answered by setting me free." (Psalm 118:5)

Women go through a lot of emotions throughout the course of a day but during a time of high stress the emotions are intensified and tend to go a *little* crazy. One minute you are happy and on track for the day. You have done your study, chores, work, and checked the mailbox. A bill comes in and suddenly you are frustrated and then tired and ultimately do not care. Within a five minute span you go from one side of the spectrum to the other...in your head.

Innocently watching a television show or movie that you thought was harmless could also trigger the rollercoaster ride. Again, you have a good and productive day. You try not to focus on the problems at hand while interacting with the kids with grace and getting dinner to the table. After dinner dishes, the family sits down to watch an evening TV show. An everyday situation is presented on the show and you flip out! It triggered an emotion that reminds you of your trial, and now you are going downhill fast with no end in sight.

How can we deal with these emotions in a healthy way?

Question: Think of an extreme betrayal or difficult situation in your life, past or present. What "triggers" or moments made you... *(Write your answers beside the emotion)*

- Angry _____
- Sad _____
- Feeling crazy _____
- Depressed _____
- Confident you'd be okay _____
- Feel nothing at all _____
- Immune or invincible _____
- Out of control crying _____

- Spiritual _____
- Panicky or anxious _____
- Other _____

The "Peace that passes all understanding" is exactly what God has generously provided for us to get through these emotions.

"And the peace of God, which transcends all understanding, will guard your hearts and your mind in Christ Jesus." (Philippians 4:7)

Question: What does God promise will guard your heart and mind?

_____

Do not get us wrong, you will go through these waves of emotion, maybe even daily, and it is normal. The focus should be on getting through them, not stuck in them. Masking or sinning in your frustration is never the answer.

Question: What are your commonly used masks? What emotions do you let others see and what emotions do you hide?

_____
_____
_____
_____
_____

Masks only provide a temporary escape. The problem is still there and compounding, waiting to rear its ugly head once again.

Consider this alternative from the bible to masking your issue...

"Let not the oppressed return dishonored;
Let the afflicted and needy praise Your name."(Psalm 74:21)

"My mouth will speak in praise of the LORD.
Let every creature praise his holy name
for ever and ever." (Psalm 145:21)

Question: What "tool" does the above scripture tell us to use?

_____

- Read the following scripture regarding praise and note the various ways to praise.

"Praise the Lord.
Praise God in his sanctuary;
praise him in his mighty heavens.
Praise him for his acts of power;
praise him for his surpassing greatness.
Praise him with the sounding of the trumpet,
praise him with the harp and lyre,
praise him with timbrel and dancing,
praise him with the strings and pipe,
praise him with the clash of cymbals,
praise him with resounding cymbals.
Let everything that has breath praise the Lord.
Praise the Lord."(Psalm 150)

- Share how and where *you* currently praise the Lord and consider incorporating a new way to praise as well.

_____
_____
_____

Action: Commit this week to begin a healthy care routine for yourself!
Choose one or two new habits to adopt such as reading daily devotions,
allotting prayer times, applying a face mask or even just taking walks.
The point is to seek healthy ways to handle the emotional rollercoaster.

Day 3, Chapter 7

Views on Family

"Wait for the Lord; be strong and take heart and wait for the Lord." (Psalm 27:14)

In the 1950s, the perfect family appeared to be one in which the mom stayed home to raise the kids while the dad worked and came home at five o'clock to a full course dinner eaten at the table. We all know that many of today's families are made up of single and working parents, fast paced full days, meals eaten in the car if at all, and technological distractions. Every time a new precedent in society is set, the family structure changes.

The situation in which you were raised greatly determines how you want to raise your family and how you handle every day and various stressful issues. Some of us want to keep up a legacy of a happy home and some of us want nothing more than a completely new family legacy to begin with us.

Question: In which family category were you raised? Circle the one that fits the best. Share your family situation.
- The 1950's family
- The divorced family
- The single parent family
- The "cover-up" family (one that looked perfect to others but was full of problems)
- Other _____

Question: How did you imagine what your family structure would look like when you were grown?

_____

_____

_____

Question: What are the differences between how you imagined your life would be and what it actually is?

Coming to grips with the reality of our past and how it affects our present and future is a step toward the realization of our new goals. You can't change the past but you can change your outlook on the future! There are blessings in our daily life that get us through each day; the smile of a child, finding a great coupon, or a perfect parking spot to name a few.

- Name some blessings that you have received. No blessing from the Father is too small!

Praise the Lord!!!

Isn't it the best feeling when a child comes to you and says thanks for dinner or a co-worker says thank you for a job well done? Our heavenly Father loves for us to recognize the things that He does for us. He wants us to enjoy the blessings.

> *"Blessed are all who fear the Lord, who walk in obedience to him. You will eat the fruit of your labor; blessings and prosperity will be yours." (Psalm 128:1-2)*

Action: Praise God this week for all of the blessings that you have as you are reminded of them daily.

Day 4, Chapter 8

The Grass is Not Always Greener on the Other Side

"But those who hope in the Lord will renew their strength. They will soar on wings as eagles; they will run and not grow weary, they will walk and not be faint. (Isaiah 40:31)

Consider the following snippet of a very important bible story from the book of Genesis: Abrahm and Lot lived in wealth and prosperity until the land could no longer support their households and they decided to part ways. Lot looked and saw a greater pasture and fertile land. It was, however, near a wicked city but he wanted it anyway. Abrahm chose the less fertile ground, away from the city. He remained faithful to God, acknowledging His glory, and God rewarded him for his loyalty and his selflessness.

- Read Ecclesiastes 7:13-14 and fill in the blanks.
  "Consider what God has done: who can straighten what he has made crooked? When times are _____, be _____; but when times are _____, _____ this: God has made the one as well as the other. Therefore, no one can discover _____ about their _____."

Question: According the above verse, what can we know about our future?

Question: In bad times do you have a tendency to blame God...even just a little? Explain or give an example.

Question: In bad times do you feel as if God is not listening to your prayers or even there? Explain.

_____

_____

_____

- Read and write Psalm 101:6 :

_____

_____

_____

God sees us when we are faithful, in bad times and good, but he dwells with us always. Of course, we need to turn our eyes to the one who is blameless. Ahhhhh… if we could only remember to do it! Along with looking at Jesus, we may need to consider who we keep company with on a daily basis. Are those you surround your life with purposing their lives to be blameless?

Question: List and contemplate those you spend the majority of your time with?

_____

_____

_____

Question: Consider the type of activities you fill your day with. Are they Christ centered or worldly focused? (i.e. television shows, radio stations, conversations, events)

_____

_____

_____

_____

You cannot control other people's choices or influences; all we can do is pray for ourselves and for them. Others may not keep good company or positive surroundings. Although some situations are out of your control such as work or school environments, it is still up to you to shield yourself and your family.

- Come up with some ideas with how you can *realistically* shield yourself and your family from these influences? Discuss.

  _____

  _____

  _____

  _____

  _____

Action: Take this week to notice positive and negative influences in your life. What steps can you take to eliminate some of the bad?

Week 3

What About Others? What About Me?

Day 1, Chapter 9

Our Sweet Children

"Her children arise and call her blessed; her husband also, and he praises her." (Proverbs 31:28)

"By faith Isaac blessed Jacob and Esau in regard to their future. By faith Jacob, when he was dying, blessed each of Joseph's sons, and worshiped as he leaned on the top of his staff." (Hebrews 11:20-21)

In the above story, Isaac blessed his sons and their futures. The result in the generations to come was that Jacob blessed his son and grandchildren as he worshipped and leaned on God. From Isaac, to Jacob, to Joseph, to Joseph's sons, the blessings continued right down the line. Isaac not only prayed blessings over them, but set an example of righteous parenthood and concern for future generations. Consider all the children in your life…from nieces, nephews, and grandchildren to children you encounter in church and other places in this section.

- Check all that apply:

We are to…

- ❏ Speak blessings over the children.
- ❏ Force our children to believe.
- ❏ Worship the Lord daily.
- ❏ Remind the children what comes around goes around.
- ❏ Tell our kids they will have to move into the backyard if they don't do their chores.
- ❏ Lean on Jesus for strength and comfort.

We are charged with praying blessings over the children as we care for ourselves by worshipping and leaning on Jesus.

- Contemplate the following verse:

"But from everlasting to everlasting the LORD's love is with those who fear him, and his righteousness with their children's children—" (Psalm 103:17)

Question: What does "everlasting to everlasting" mean in above scripture?

_____

_____

_____

No matter what our situation is or how we feel at the time, regardless of a wayward spouse, sibling or child, we need to claim these blessings for our children and our children's children. The example we set is the example we hope they will continue down the line.

"This day I call the heavens and the earth as witnesses against you that I have set before you life and death, blessings and curses. Now choose life, so that you and your children may live and that you may love the LORD your God, listen to his voice, and hold fast to him. For the LORD is your life, and he will give you many years in the land he swore to give to your fathers, Abraham, Isaac and Jacob." (Deuteronomy 30:19-20)

• List the four commands the above scripture is asking us to do. Discuss.

1. _____

2. _____

3. _____

4. _____

Action: "Finally, brothers and sisters, whatever is true, whatever is noble, whatever is right, whatever is pure, whatever is lovely, whatever is admirable—if anything is excellent or praiseworthy—think about such things." (Philippians 4:8)

Day 2, Chapter 10

Revenge

"Be still before the LORD and wait patiently for him;
fret not yourself over the one who prospers in his way,
over the man who carries out evil devises! Refrain from
anger, and forsake wrath! Fret not yourself; it tends only
to evil. For the evildoer shall be cut off, but those who
wait for the LORD shall inherit the land." (Psalm 37:7-9)

Let's not mince words on this subject; let's dive right in. The bible is
very clear on revenge, but we do not see it clearly sometimes. We have
all thought about seeking revenge from the simplest things like wanting
to squish an ant for biting you to the life altering events such as seeking
retribution from a spousal betrayal.

Question: Have you ever reacted to something in a vengeful way? How
did that turn out for ya? Explain.

Have you ever thought about the small emotions that lead to a larger
feeling to take revenge? Revenge is even in the words we speak; those
little jabs.

- Examine your heart for a moment and share an example of the
  little words that have large consequences.

- Read Ephesians 4:31-32

*"Get rid of all **bitterness**, **rage**, and **anger**, **brawling** and **slander**, along with every form of **malice**. Be kind and compassionate to one another, forgiving each other, just as in Christ God forgave you." (Ephesians 4:31-32)*

- Define in your own words and in your own life the following:
    - Bitterness _____
    - Rage _____
    - Anger _____
    - Brawling _____
    - Slander _____
    - Malice _____

Question: Is their one of the preceding words that you particularly struggle with that you would like to discuss further with the group?

_____

_____

_____

- Re-read the introductory verse, Psalm 37:7-9 and fill in the blanks.

"Be _____ before the Lord and _____ for him; _____ yourself over the one who prospers in his way, over the man who carries out evil devices! _____ from anger, and _____ wrath! _____ yourself; it tends only to evil. For the evil doer shall be cut off, but those who _____ for the LORD _____ inherit the land." (Psalm 37:7-9)

Question: We are to <u>what</u> for him?

We are to _____ and we are not to_____. The verse mentions these two verbs twice. We are pretty sure that if something is mentioned more than once we should definitely take note. On the other hand, we are also pretty sure that these things seem quite impossible to do when in the midst of a crisis. Let's examine some of the words in the passage above so we can fully comprehend God's meaning. What do the following words mean to you?

- To be still _____
- To wait _____
- To be patient _____
- To fret not _____

Realistically, how are we supposed to be patient and wait for the Lord? Well, we have only but to stand on the promises of God. Here are a few promises, but thankfully there are so many more! (See Chapter 13 for more examples to reference.)

> *"I remain confident of this: I will see the goodness of the Lord in the land of the living. **Wait** for the Lord; be strong and take heart and **wait** for the Lord." (Psalm 27:13-14)*

> *"Through patience a ruler can be persuaded, and a gentle tongue can break a bone." (Proverbs 25:15)*

The Lord knows exactly what we are thinking, what is in our hearts, and on our minds. It is normal to have these feelings and to want to protect your life and your family. We just need to refrain from repaying evil for evil and leave the revenge to God.

Action: Catch yourself this week in acts of subtle revenge. For each occurrence, recognize it and give it up to the Lord. Confess your thoughts, good and bad, to the Lord in prayer.

Day 3, Chapter 11

Open Your Eyes to God's Blessings "Amidst the Storm"

"When the storm has swept by, the wicked are gone, but the righteous stand firm forever." (Proverbs 10:25)

- Look up 2 Corinthians 4:16-17 and fill in the blanks.

"Therefore we do not lose _____. Though _____ we are wasting away, yet _____ we are being renewed day by day. For our light and _____ are achieving for us an eternal glory that far _____ them all."

We know our physical bodies are only temporary and during a crisis the evidence of physical deterioration becomes more noticeable. You may feel like your face droops, your smile is gone, and your body is tired.

- Check all that apply:
    - ❏ Droopy face
    - ❏ Slouched shoulders
    - ❏ Voluminous hair
    - ❏ Wrinkles
    - ❏ Spring in your step
    - ❏ Other _____

Thank you Jesus! The Lord gives us hope that even though our outside appears to be wasting away our inside is being renewed daily. His renewal is supernatural and can't be lifted by a visit to the plastic surgeon.

Question: What SITUATIONS or WHO are you "losing heart" in or giving up on?

_____
_____
_____

Question: What are some ways you can let God renew your spirit daily?

_____

_____

_____

We know we tend to harp on this subject but all of us neglect ourselves too often. It is an important daily ritual to allow God to renew your spirit. Take time for yourself *and* for the Lord.

In 2 Corinthians 4:16-17, it is mentioned that our troubles are momentary and an eternal glory waits. Life is short. Even though we lose heart in the midst of adversity, remember there is a light at the end of every tunnel. Don't miss the blessings along the way. Don't miss what God is trying to show you or have you learn.

Action: Take some time this week to read the book of Job and remember how the Lord renewed and restored him. Journal how the Lord speaks to you through the book of Job.

_____

_____

_____

_____

_____

_____

_____

_____

_____

_____

_____

_____

_____

_____

_____

Day 4, Chapter 12

Inner Beauty

"Charm is deceptive, and beauty is fleeting; but a woman who fears the Lord is to be praised. Give her the reward she has earned, and let her works bring her praise at the city gate." (Proverbs 31:30-31)

What attracts people to you as you are today? Do you have depth of character? Are you a pleasing person to know or a sourpuss? Is empathy your forte, or your intellect? Are you a creative person, a leader, or an excellent servant? Who are you when you are at your best?

We all know that outer beauty is fleeting but strength of character and morality builds inner beauty that is lasting.

That said, our care in our appearance often tells of our spiritual health. You may have heard the saying that a messy environment equals a messy life. Now that is not always true. Sometimes it means a creative life, or a busy life, etc…

The word says:

"So from now on we regard no one from a worldly point of view." (2 Corinthians 5:16a)

And it continues on:

"Therefore, if anyone is in Christ, he is a new creation; the old has gone, the new has come!" (2 Corinthians 5:17)

No matter what your life looks like from an outside view, creating inner beauty starts by becoming a new creation in Christ. As a new creation, walking alone in your struggles is virtually impossible! Jesus longs to come beside us and hold our hand. His presence makes us beautiful because His love is perfect. When we walk with Christ we begin a new life. Some of us may need to go back and remind ourselves of whom we are in Christ and who God made us to be.

Question: Who do you think you are in God's eyes?

Group Challenge: Take an index card and put your name on it. Pass them in to the leader and draw another name from a bowl. Anonymously, describe on the card the person on the card's positive character traits as you see them. Return the card to the bowl and the leader will return your card to you. (The leader could instead read the comments aloud and have people guess who that is.)

> **Question:** What do the words on the card reflect about you? Are you displaying what the Lord wants others to see in you or what you want others to see? Do you feel the words on the card accurately describe your inner beauty rather than your physical attributes?
>
> ---
>
> ---
>
> ---

Individual Challenge: Ask a family member or a friend to tell you your positive attributes. Examine your heart and how those attributes reflect you.

> **Question:** Are you displaying what the Lord wants others to see in you or what you want others to see?
>
> ---
>
> ---
>
> ---

> **Question:** How does this reflect your inner beauty rather than your outward appearance?
>
> ---
>
> ---
>
> ---

Because God cherishes you, you should cherish yourself. As a new creation, the Holy Spirit brings us new purpose and inner character that is perfected as you seek His will. Remember...

> *"Charm is deceptive, and beauty is fleeting; but a woman who fears the Lord is to be praised." (Proverbs 31:30)*

Extra: Read on your own the story of the Proverbs 31 woman, located in Proverbs 31:10-31. Remember she is attractive because of her character, not because of her outward beauty. She is a model of multiple positive character qualities to aspire to. The Lord blesses us each with some of these traits to grow and improve upon, making us the person He intends for us to be.

Action: Commit or recommit yourself to the Lord, if you feel the Holy Spirit urging you. Start today grooming your inner beauty to be a light to others in your life.

Week 4

His Perfect Plan

Day 1, Chapter 13

God's Promises

"Commit yourself to the Lord whatever you do
and your plans will succeed." (Proverbs 16:3)

"God promises abundant blessings if we meet with
Him daily, pray fervently, meditate on His word, and
share with others." (Lynn and Christine, 2013).

Time and perseverance…You must go through the process and not be rescued from the emotional ups and downs until it is time or you will miss what God has for you to learn. God desires to bless us and to help us grow spiritually. Diving into His word and recognizing His promises gives us comfort, direction, and goals. He wants to make each of us an example of His glory and pass that heritage down to future generations.

God promises abundant blessings if we meet with Him daily, pray fervently, meditate on His word, and share with others. It is *never too late* to begin walking a God-driven path of righteousness. It is okay to stumble and fall along that path as long as we pick ourselves up, dust ourselves off, and keep moving forward. Lord knows, we have had to pick ourselves and each other off of the floor MANY times along the way.

There are so many blessings in the Bible that it would be impossible to list them all. Together we have chosen some of the verses and organized them into manageable and familiar subtopics that we feel are applicable to our lives at this time.

For this section, we hope you can take some quiet time to read and dwell on each passage. Feel free to comment on which scripture impacted you the most on the lines provided under each of the promise sections.

As a group: Divvy up the sections during the group bible study time and then gather to discuss the comments. This exercise could utilize more than one meeting time.

As an individual: We feel it would be beneficial to comment on all of the sections which may take more than one sitting but if you are pressed for time, cover as many as you can.

Destroy the Power of the Enemy

"God blesses those who are kind to the poor and helpless.
He helps them out of their own troubles. He protects
them and keeps them alive; he publicly honors them and
destroys the power of their enemies." (Psalm 41:1-2)

"If you return to the Almighty, you will be blessed
again. So remove evil from your house."
(Job 22:23 NCV)

"Blessed is the man who always fears the Lord but
he who hardens his heart falls into trouble."
(Proverbs 28:14)

Comments:

Blessings

"Blessed is the man who perseveres under trial, because when
he has stood the test, he will receive the crown of life that
God has promised to those who love him." (James 1:12)

"But even if you should suffer for what is right,
you are blessed." (1 Peter 3:14a)

"If you are insulted because of the name of Christ, you are blessed,
for the Spirit of glory and of God rests on you." (1 Peter 4:14)

Comments:

_____

_____

_____

Grace

"From the fullness of his grace we have all received
one blessing after another." (John 1:16)

"The Lord longs to be gracious to you; he rises to show
you compassion. For the Lord is a God of justice. Blessed
are all who wait for him!" (Isaiah 30:18)

Comments:

_____

_____

_____

Fellowship

"I will enjoy blessing them. With all my heart and soul I will
faithfully plant them in this land." (Jeremiah 32:41 GW)

"I'm eager to encourage you in your faith, but I also
want to be encouraged by yours. In this way, each of us
will be a blessing to the other." (Rom 1:12 NLT)

"It is more blessed to give than to receive." (Acts 20:35)
"Blessed is the man who finds wisdom and
gains understanding." (Proverbs 3:13)

Comments:

_____

_____

_____

Financial

"A generous man will himself be blessed, for he
shares his food with the poor." (Proverbs 22:9)

"A faithful man will be richly blessed, but one eager to
get rich will not go unpunished." (Proverbs 28:20)

"People curse the man who hoards grain, but
blessing crowns him who is willing to sell."
(Proverbs 11:26)

"Bring the whole tithe into the storehouse, that there may be food
in my house. 'Test me in this,' says the Lord Almighty, 'and see if I
will not throw open the floodgates of heaven and pour out so much
blessing that you will not have room enough for it.'" (Malachi 3:10)

Comments:

_____

_____

_____

Material Blessings

"All these blessings will come on you and accompany you if you
obey the LORD your God: You will be blessed in the city and
blessed in the country. The fruit of your womb will be blessed,
and the crops of your land and the young of your livestock—the
calves of your herds and the lambs of your flocks. Your basket and
your kneading trough will be blessed. You will be blessed when
you come in and blessed when you go out. The LORD will grant
that the enemies who rise up against you will be defeated before
you. They will come at you from one direction but flee from you
in seven. The LORD will send a blessing on your barns and on
everything you put your hand to. The LORD your God will bless
you in the land he is giving you." (Deuteronomy 28:2-8 NLT)

"I will cause my people and their homes around my holy hill to be a blessing. And I will send showers, showers of blessings, which will come just when they are needed." (Ezekiel 34:26 NLT)

"The Lord blessed Job in the second half of his life even more than in the first half of his life." (Job 42:12)

Comments:

_____

_____

_____

Protection

"Lord, you have stored up great blessings for those who honor you. You do much for those who come to you for protection, blessing them before the watching world." (Psalm 31:19 NLT)

"Blessed is he who has regard for the weak; the Lord delivers him in times of trouble. The Lord will protect him and preserve his life; he will bless him in the land and not surrender him to the desire of his foes." (Psalm 41:1-2)

"The Lord's curse is on the house of the wicked, but he blesses the home of the righteous." (Proverbs 3:33)

Comments:

_____

_____

_____

Generations

"After Abraham's death, God poured out rich blessings on Isaac." (Gen. 25:11 NLT)

"For those who are always generous and lend freely,
their children will be blessed." (Psalm 37:26)

"Blessed is the man who fears the Lord, who finds great delight in his
commands. His children will be mighty in the land; the generation of
the upright will be blessed. Wealth and riches are in his house, and his
righteousness endures forever. Even in darkness light dawns for the
upright, for the gracious and compassionate and righteous man. Good
will come to him who is generous and lends freely, who conducts
his affairs with justice. Surely he will never be shaken; a righteous
man will be remembered forever. He will have no fear of bad news;
his heart is steadfast, trusting in the Lord. His heart is secure, he
will have no fear; in the end he will look in triumph on his foes. He
has scattered abroad his gifts to the poor, his righteousness endures
forever; his horn will be lifted high in honor." (Psalm 112:1-9)

"The memory of the righteous will be a blessing." (Proverbs 10:7)

Comments:

Daily Faithfulness

"Jesus said, 'Blessed are those who have not seen
me and yet have believed.'" (John 20:29)

"Blessed is the man who trusts in you." (Psalm 84:12)

"I pray that your partnership with us in the faith may be
effective in deepening your understanding of every good
thing we share for the sake of Christ." (Philemon 1:6)

"The one who plants and the one who waters have one
purpose, and they will each be rewarded according
to their own labor." (1 Corinthians. 3:8)

"Blessed is the one who does not walk in step with
the wicked or stand in the way that sinners take or
sit in the company of mockers." (Psalm 1:1)

"Do not repay evil with evil or insult with insult,
but with blessing, because to this you were called so
that you may inherit a blessing." (1 Peter 3:9)

"Blessed is the man who makes the Lord his trust, who does not look
to the proud, to those who turn aside to false gods." (Psalm 40:4)

"Blessed are all who fear the Lord, who
walk in his ways." (Psalm 128:1)

"Blessed is the man who trusts in the Lord, whose
confidence is in him." (Jeremiah 17:7)

"He who pursues righteousness and love finds life,
prosperity and honor." (Proverbs 21:21)

Comments:

_____

_____

_____

From the Word

"Blessed are those who hear the word of
God and obey it." (Luke 11:28)

"Even more blessed are all who hear the word of God
and put it into practice." (Luke 11:28 NLT)

"The man who looks intently into the perfect law that gives
freedom, and continues to do this, not forgetting what he has heard,
but doing it – he will be blessed in what he does." (James 1:25)

"Blessed is the man... whose delight is in the law of the Lord, and on his word he meditates day and night. He is like a tree planted by streams of water, which yields its fruit in season and whose leaf does not wither. Whatever he does prospers." (Psalm 1:1-3)

"Do not turn aside from any of the commands I give you today, to the right or to the left, following other gods and serving them." (Deuteronomy 28:14)

"Whoever gives heed to instruction prospers, and blessed is he who trusts in the Lord." (Proverbs 16:20)

Comments:

_____

_____

_____

Praise

"Praise be to the God and Father of our Lord Jesus Christ, who has blessed us in the heavenly realms with every spiritual blessing in Christ." (Ephesians 1:3)

"Blessed are the poor in spirit, for theirs is the kingdom of heaven. Blessed are those who mourn, for they will be comforted. Blessed are the meek, for they will inherit the earth. Blessed are those who hunger and thirst for righteousness, for they will be filled. Blessed are the merciful, for they will be shown mercy. Blessed are the pure in heart, for they will see God. Blessed are the peacemakers, for they will be called sons of God. Blessed are those who are persecuted because of righteousness, for theirs is the kingdom of heaven. Blessed are you when people insult you, persecute you and falsely say all kinds of evil against you because of me." (Matthew 5:3-11)

"Now that you know these things, you will be
blessed if you do them." (John 13:17)

Comments:

_____

_____

_____

Action: Think of something you can do that will put scripture in your life on a daily basis. Download an app, cut and paste a verse and put it on a mirror…whatever it takes to immerse yourself in the word daily.

Day 2, Chapter 14

Understanding What They are Going Through

"For all have sinned and fall short of the
glory of God." (Romans 3:23)

Understanding....hmmm. That is a rough subject when you have been hurt to the point of despair. However, there is always another side of the story. We may not want to find out what that is or even care but unless we do we may not be able to heal, and we definitely want healing! True, there are no excuses for certain things or behaviors but we need to move forward and not backwards, with God's help. The bible says this: *"And you must show mercy to those whose faith is wavering." (Jude 1:22)*

- Name a time you needed to show mercy to another.

  _____

  _____

  _____

  (I do know that when I have had to show mercy a time or two I felt like the Lord was behind me pushing the words and actions out, ugh!)

  Why must we show mercy, when we feel the other person does not deserve it? Simply put, the bible tells us to, and that is reason enough.

  Okay moving on... scenarios...your brother commits murder or you tell a lie to not have to go to an event. Big sin little sin, is there a difference? To us, there is a huge difference and we justify our "little" lie over and over again until it becomes the truth to us. Let's remember, in the eyes of the Lord there is no difference.

- Discuss "big sin, little sin".

  _____

  _____

  _____

- Read and write 1 John 1:8-10 on the following lines.

  _____
  _____
  _____
  _____
  _____
  _____

Once we identify our personal sins of any kind and confess them, our prayer line to God is open and powerful. You may not have the blame in the situation you are facing, but when we dig deep, our sins begin to surface, and we are able to clear our hearts and minds of any wrong thinking.

- Fill in the blanks.

  _"Therefore _____ to each other and pray for each other so that _____. The prayer of a _____ person is powerful and effective." (James 5:16)_

Once our hearts are right and we have confessed our sins we can begin the healing process and show others the glory of God. After all, we are put on this earth to bring glory to God through the gift of His salvation. We can use our struggles to positively affect change in others. As our hearts begin to change, others will see the Lord's care for us.

> **_Action: Take time this week to identify your sins and then confess them in prayer. Think of a way you can turn your situation into an example of God's glory for others to see._**

Day 3, Chapter 15

God's Timing

"The Lord is not slow in keeping his promise, as some understand slowness. He is patient with you, not wanting anyone to perish, but everyone to come to repentance." (2Peter 3:9)

- *MAD LIB TIME! Wahoo!*

Place a noun in each of the blanks and then reread. Share if you want.

A _____ for Everything
"There is a _____ for everything,
and a season for every activity under the heavens:
a _____ to be born and a _____ to die,
a _____ to plant and a _____ to uproot,
a _____ to kill and a _____ to heal,
a _____ to tear down and a _____ to build,
a _____ to weep and a _____ to laugh,
a _____ to mourn and a _____ to dance,
a _____ to scatter stones and a _____ to gather them,
a _____ to embrace and a _____ to refrain from
embracing,
a _____ to search and a _____ to give up,
a _____ to keep and a _____ to throw away,
a _____ to tear and a _____ to mend,
a _____ to be silent and a _____ to speak,
a _____ to love and a _____ to hate,
a _____ for war and a _____ for
peace. (Ecclesiastes 3:1-8)

Now replace all of the blanks with the word "time". Count how many times the word "time" is used in the above passage. Answer: _____.

Question: Why do you think the word "time" is used repeatedly?

_____

_____

_____

We assuredly have "time" issues. If something takes too long then we start thinking about what we are doing next or get frustrated. There seems to not be enough time for the things we want to do but way too much time for the things we don't want to do. We also want all our prayers answered instantaneously. Yes, we definitely have "time" issues!

- Let's read a few more verses…

"What do workers gain from their toil? I have seen the burden God has laid on the human race. He has made everything beautiful in its time. He has also set eternity in the human heart; yet no one can fathom what God has done from beginning to end. I know that there is nothing better for people than to be happy and to do good while they live. That each of them may eat and drink, and find satisfaction in all their toil—this is the gift of God." (Ecclesiastes 3:9-13)

Some issues are resolved quickly like praying for financial matters and being handed a check minutes later, while other issues seem to drag on forever like healing from cancer treatments or a broken marriage.

Question: Can you name a time when your prayer was answered quickly?

_____

_____

_____

Question: Tell about an instance when your answer took a much longer time.

_____

_____

_____

2 Peter 3:8 says: *"But do not forget this one thing, dear friends: With the Lord a day is like a thousand years, and a thousand years are like a day."* And again in Psalm 90:4 the word says *"A thousand years in your sight are like a day that has just gone by, or like a watch in the night."* Our time is hardly ever God's time. Because God is omniscient, He can see how all things work together in His perfect plan. There may be something else that needs to happen first before your prayers are answered according to His ultimate wisdom.

Action: Ask God to show you areas where time is an issue in your life. Pray for a better understanding of what it means to wait on the Lord. Trust that the Lord has a perfect plan for you.

Day 4, Chapter 16

Our Story: Your Story

"I have told you these things, so that in me you may
have peace. In this world you will have trouble. But
take heart! I have overcome the world." (John 16:33)

In the above verse, Jesus tells us that he has already overcome the world yet sometimes it feels like our problems are insurmountable. In the book, *The Rose Garden and the Ring*, Chapter 16 tells Lynn and Christine's story of the beginning of their restoration. We would like to give you the time and space to reflect on *your* story.

- Take a few moments to journal whatever you are facing at the moment.

_____

_____

_____

_____

_____

_____

_____

_____

_____

_____

Question: Now that you have written it all out, where are you hoping to be in a year?

_____

_____

_____

_____

As Jesus was preparing himself and his disciples for the cross, he instructed them in John 16:24 *"Until now you have not asked for anything in my name. Ask and you will receive, and your joy will be complete."*

- Construct your own prayer asking whatever you need in Jesus' name. Remember to confess your sins first and give thanks for His provision in your life.

Action: We encourage you to go back and write in the journal and prayer section in today's lesson if you skipped it ☺. Consider keeping your own journal at home.

Week 5

God's Work

Day 1, Chapter 17

That "Forgiveness" Word

"If my people, who are called by my name, will humble themselves and pray and seek my face and turn from their wicked ways, then I will hear from heaven, and I will forgive their sin and will heal their land." (2 Chronicles 7:14)

Approaching this topic arouses a whole host of emotions and avoidances. Releasing forgiveness to another deals with giving up the resentment towards that person. Let it be said again and again, it is not a release of guilt or responsibility from you or another person. Forgiving is simply an acknowledgement of the wrong that has been done to you and a decision to move forward with healing. Sometimes you even have to forgive yourself from what you have done to yourself. Forgiveness is a very humbling process because we have to put away our pride whether we need to forgive or be forgiven.

Question: Is there anyone you need to forgive? If so, who and why?

_____

_____

_____

Question: Does pride get in the way of <u>your</u> forgiveness process?

_____

_____

_____

Question: What else gets in the way of forgiveness in your life?

_____

_____

_____

I am perfect. Just kidding… no one is "perfect". Not even one. Soooooo…

Question: Is there something you need to forgive yourself for?

_____

_____

_____

What if a person does not ask for forgiveness? What do you do then? You can't change the past, and harboring the bitterness and unforgiveness only hurts you! Unfortunately, while digging deeper on this subject, we realized that the only way <u>we</u> could forgive a person who wronged us was to go back in time and make that person never have hurt us in the first place. That is not going to happen and so, based on this logic, we will never forgive. _That thinking must change._ The past is not going to change. We should forgive and move on rather than wait eternally for the past to be reconstructed. Remember that forgiveness is not always for them, but for you and your walk with Jesus.

- Fill in the blanks

"_____ you forgive _____. And what I have forgiven-if there was to forgive-I have forgiven in the sight of Christ, in order that _____ might not outwit us. For we are not unaware of _____." (2 Corinthians 2:10-11)

If we don't forgive, we open the door for Satan to gain a foothold. He can use our anger and bitterness against us and let it spread like a virus. We must forgive and be forgiven to foil Satan's plan, thus ultimately benefitting ourselves and others.

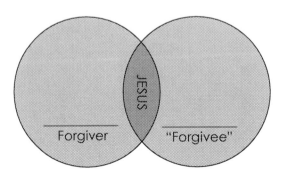

Jesus is the bond that ties our forgiveness together. His forgiveness was accomplished on the cross. Who are we to not forgive? Although it is a daunting task, the Lord gives us plenty of reason to forgive others as He has forgiven us. We understand it is easier said than done, but forgiveness WILL set you free. God's will is perfect.

- Stop right now and give your unforgiveness to God in prayer. Release it to His mighty power and perfect plan.

Action: Pour blessings into the life of another by praying for forgiveness for them and for yourself!

Repercussions, Triggers and the Tongue

"Let us not become weary in doing good,
for at the proper time we will reap a harvest
if we do not give up." (Galatians 6:9)

We absolutely love this verse! Therefore, here it is again… "Let us not become weary in doing good, for at the proper time we will reap a harvest if we do not give up." (Galatians 6:9)

(your name), don't give up! Did you hear us? Say it out loud… *(your name)*, DON'T GIVE UP!

Before we get too far into this topic, consider what God is saying in the book of Job:

"So listen to me, you men of understanding. Far be it from God to do evil, from the Almighty to do wrong. He repays everyone for what they have done; he brings on them what their conduct deserves." (Job 34:10-11)

This verse is saying that God does not inflict evil upon us. However, there are consequences to our actions. Our own actions and the actions of others dictate our repercussions. Even though we may not be doing anything wrong, we can still suffer consequences from someone else's actions

We call the fallout from past actions taken "triggers". It seems as though those triggers, which are different for every person, will set you off down the wrong path because they remind you of the pain caused by what happened to you in your life. Examples of a trigger may include a certain movie theme, a simple cell phone call, or a certain song on the radio. You can't avoid them but your reaction can be managed.

Question: What are your "triggers"?

_____

_____

Exhibiting self-control when a trigger occurs could make a huge difference. Some of the ways we found helpful are to immediately be calm and quiet while taking a few deep breaths or to just leave the room before you "lose it". Practice makes perfect so if you fail or your techniques do not work just keep trying!

Question: What additional techniques can _you_ use to manage the triggers?

_____

_____

The normal reaction to a trigger is "open mouth, insert foot." The Lord speaks often about the potential harm our words can cause. A popular "Christianese" response to sharp words is "taming the tongue"…does that strike a nerve?

- Read and ponder the contents of James 3 on taming the tongue. Answer the following questions.

Questions:
How do you tame a horse? _____
How do you steer a ship? _____
How is a forest fire started? _____
Where does our praise come from? _____
Where do curses come from? _____
Can the tongue be tamed? _____

James 3:8 says it best. The tongue cannot be tamed but is "a restless evil full of deadly poison". We can only pray we have enough self-control when the time comes.

Action: Make an earnest effort this week to tame your tongue over and over again and ask for forgiveness when you stumble.

Day 3, Chapter 19

Miracles

"You are the God who performs miracles; you display your power among the peoples." (Psalm 77:14)

Sitting at a church-wide dinner to raise money for the debt on our new building, the pastor was talking about the difference between a tithe and an offering. The Holy Spirit spoke to me and said, "I want you to make a commitment to tithing." My distressed reply was that my husband has left me; I have two small children and am pregnant with a third. There is a woman after my husband and his money and I don't know where my next meal will come from. Lord, how can I accept this challenge? The Lord continued to press me and asked me to give $200 a month. I said to the Holy Spirit "If you show it to me, I will give it." At the end of the banquet, a man who only knew me because I was in the choir came to me and handed me a check for $200 and told me that while he was ironing his shirt, preparing to come for the evening, the Lord said to him to give the money to me. I turned around and put the money in the offering plate the very next Sunday! That *is* a miracle.

My son caught a cold and got better in seven days. Most likely for the majority, that is not a miracle.

Question: What defines a miracle?

• Examine the following two verses.

*"He **did** miracles in the sight of their **ancestors** in the land of **Egypt**, in the region of Zoan." (Psalm 78:12).*

*"You **are** the God who **performs** miracles; you **display** your power among the peoples." (Psalm 77:14)*

The first verse is in past tense while the second verse is in present tense yet they are found in the same book of bible. If the word of God is relevant today, tomorrow, and yesterday then he *continues* to perform miracles.

Question: How do we receive those miracles?

- Fill in the blanks from Matthew 17:14-20.

"When they came to the crowd, a man approached Jesus and knelt before him. 'Lord, _____ on my son,' he said. 'He has seizures and is suffering greatly. He often falls into the fire or into the water. I brought him to your _____, but they _____ heal him.'

'You unbelieving and perverse generation,' Jesus replied, '_____ shall I stay with you? _____ should I put up with you? Bring the boy here to me." Jesus rebuked the demon, and it came out of the boy, and he was healed _____.
Then the disciples came to Jesus in private and asked, '_____'
He replied, 'Because you have _____. Truly I tell you, if you have _____ as small as a mustard seed, you can say to this mountain, move from here to there, and it will move. Nothing will be impossible for you.'"

We feel that is important to note that even the disciples struggled with the concept of miracles. But Jesus quickly rebuked them and said miracles are dependent on their faith. The faith is not in the disciples own ability to believe in miracles but that God is powerful enough to do it.

Remember that it is the Lord's decision whether that mountain really needs to be moved. After all, we are not talking about telekinesis. The miracles depend on God's will for the mountain to move and our faith in God's discernment on whether that mountain should move. In other words, our faith is in God, not the mountain and our own abilities.

Question: What are some ways a person can acquire the faith that moves mountains?

Question: How do you personally grow your faith?

- Write Romans 10:17 in the space below.

We hear it said that you don't have to go to church to be a Christian but Romans 10:17 says that faith comes through hearing, and hearing the word of Christ. Therefore whether it is from a sermon, a television show, or a radio program, our faith can be increased by hearing the word.

Action: Find a way this week to increase your "hearing" the word of God.

Day 4, Chapter 20

Updates

"Consider it pure joy, my brothers and sisters, whenever you face trials of many kinds because you know that the testing of your faith produces perseverance. Let perseverance finish its work so that you may be mature and complete, not lacking anything" (James 1:2-4)

Maturity and completeness are some things we all strive to achieve. How do we do that? This chapter allows for continued growth. We will be looking at the previous 19 chapter's "action" items.

- Choose at least three of the "Action" challenges from the following.
- Select based on your successes, flops, and do overs and list them in the area provided after Action number 19.

We would like to give you the opportunity to share what worked for you, what absolutely did not work for you, and what you want a second chance on.

Actions

1. Call out to God. You can tell Him anything. Know that the Lord is faithful. Choose to listen and learn God's word.
2. The Lord wants to lead us safely through our trials. Let him! Ask God through the Holy Spirit to guide you every day.
3. Rely on God's strength, integrity and ability. Present your plans and thoughts to God for approval whether in writing and prayer or simply with prayer. Your answer may not make sense, but God is in control and He sees the bigger picture.
4. Make your choice. Choose to give your situation to God or keep it. Then...Own it!

5. Pray this scripture daily: "Teach me to do your will for you are my God. May your gracious spirit lead me forward on a firm footing." (Psalm 143:10 NLT)

6. Commit this week to begin a healthy care routine for you! Choose one or two new habits to adopt such as reading daily devotions, allotting prayer times, applying a face mask or even just taking a walk. The point is to seek healthy ways to handle the emotional rollercoaster.

7. Praise God this week for all of the blessings that you have as you are reminded of them daily.

8. Take this week to notice positive and negative influences in your life. What steps can you take to eliminate some of the bad?

9. "Finally, brothers and sisters, whatever is true, whatever is noble, whatever is right, whatever is pure, whatever is lovely, whatever is admirable-if anything is excellent or praiseworthy-think about such things." (Philippians 4:8)

10. Catch yourself this week in acts of subtle revenge. Recognize it and give it up to the Lord immediately. Confess your thoughts, good and bad, in prayer.

11. Take some time this week to read the book of Job and remember how the Lord renewed and restored him. Journal how the Lord speaks to you through the book of Job.

12. Commit or recommit yourself to the Lord, if you feel the Holy Spirit urging you. Start today grooming your inner beauty to be a light to others in your life.

13. Think of something you can do that will put scripture in your life on a daily basis. Download an app, cut and paste a verse and put it on a mirror...whatever it takes to immerse yourself in the word daily.

14. Take time this week to identify your sins and then confess them in prayer. Think of a way you can turn your situation into an example for God's glory for others to see.

15. Ask God to show you areas where time is an issue in your life. Pray for a better understanding of what it means to wait on the Lord. Trust that the Lord has a perfect plan for you.

16. We encourage you to go back and write in the journal and prayer section in chapter 16 if you skipped it. ☺ Consider keeping a journal of your own at home.

17. Pour blessings into the life of another by praying for forgiveness for them and for yourself!

18. Make an earnest effort this week to tame your tongue over and over again and ask for forgiveness when you stumble.

19. Find a way this week to increase your "hearing" the word of God.

My SUCCESSFUL Actions:

_____

_____

_____

_____

_____

My FLOPPED Actions:

_____

_____

_____

_____

_____

What I want to DO OVER:

_____

_____

_____

_____

_____

No-one is perfect; we have to revisit these things on a constant basis. Share with the group or with another person your findings.

Action: Ask someone to hold you accountable to the "Actions" you have committed to revisit or follow through on.

Week 6

Reaching

Day 1, Chapter 21

Your Story: Your Witness

"As iron sharpens iron, so one person
sharpens another." (Proverbs 27:17)

"Therefore I urge you, brothers and sisters, in view
of God's mercy, to offer your bodies as a living
sacrifice, holy and pleasing to God – this is your
true and proper worship." (Romans 12:1)

As we encourage one another, share what works for you in your current phase of life. Many might feel that sharing is inappropriate, or that our problems are personal. Where that is sometimes true, sharing with each other will help show our humanity as well as our spiritual side. Enjoy your "true worship" time as you edify one another in Christ!

Have you ever had a chance to share your testimony? Well…here you go! A true testimony is a public telling of a faith based experience. We would like to give you this opportunity to write it out. What has God done for you? How did you come to know Christ? Were you "delivered" from any situation? Who were you before knowing the Lord?

Your Testimony:

_____

_____

_____

_____

_____

_____

_____

_____

_____

_____

Question: Would your testimony help anyone else if you had the opportunity to share?

Question: In what ways would it spark conversation and encourage healing?

"But in your hearts revere Christ as Lord. Always be prepared to give an answer to everyone who asks you to give the reason for the hope that you have. But do this with gentleness and respect." (1 Peter 3:15)

"Let the redeemed of the Lord tell their story-those he redeemed from the hand of the foe [Satan]." (Psalm 107:2)

Action: If you feel willing, ready and able to share your testimony with a group or with an individual, please do so at this time.

Day 2, Chapter 22

From us Girls - The New You

"For I know the plans I have for you," declares the
LORD, "plans to prosper you and not to harm you, plans
to give you hope and a future." (Jeremiah 29:11)

We are so blessed that you have made it to the end of this study. Hopefully we have been transparent enough to have walked along side you throughout this journey. One thing is for sure, your experiences and struggles have changed you. For example, whether it is the death of someone close to you, a broken marriage, or a child leaving home, we are led to finding a way to live without that person. Physical or emotional abandonment most often leads to fighting major self-worth issues. Also, any change in a job (mother, wife, executive) revamps daily routines.

You may like this new person you have become or you may not. You may only like just parts of "you" now, but dislike other aspects.

Question: What does the "new you" look like?

_____

_____

_____

If the "new you" involves harboring resentment, feeling depressed all of the time, or lacking in hope or self-worth, something else needs to change. Think about what or who needs to change.

Question: What could be causing you continued distress?

_____

_____

_____

We have mentioned many times in this study guide that the way you view life can be altered. Yes, people can change but only if THEY want to. You can't change them. You can only change yourself. In each and every situation try finding the bright spots and the blessings and avoid dwelling on the negative or difficult. See the good more than the pain. The Lord honors our efforts; this can be a start.

"A cheerful heart is good medicine, but a crushed spirit dries up the bones." (Proverbs 17:22)

Question: What are some other ways you are willing to make a change for the better? What situations need altered and how can you change them to achieve a happier, healthier life? (Remember...all things are possible with Christ)

No life is ever going to be absolutely perfect and without challenges. But you have the ability and power, with God's help, to make positive changes that will affect your future. Perhaps the change involves forgiveness; it will not be easy. Dwelling on the past seems inevitable but maybe instead of dwelling just remember the past, focus on the good that came out of it no matter how small, and charge into the future.

Remember we started this bible study with a decision...Are you going to include God in your life and follow the path He has for you or not? Let us close with a decision...Are you going to let God help you focus on your gifts and get out of any pit you may be in or not?

Action: Make a decision...Are you going to let God help you focus on your gifts and get out of any pit you may be in or not?

Day 3, Chapter 23

From the Mouths of Babes

"'Do you hear what these children are saying?'
they asked him. 'Yes,' replied Jesus, 'have you never
read, from the lips of children and infants you, Lord,
have called forth your praise'?" (Matthew 21:16)

The youth of today are the adults of tomorrow. If they are constantly faced with struggles and focus their attention on the bad, then where is their hope? As family or friends of the family, we should remind them of God's miracles, big and small, occurring around them every day. Youth have a unique perspective of faith and miracles that adults often overlook.

The following represent a few examples of miracles and incidences in which they knew God was with them that our children will always remember.

Through the eyes of a child:

Youth A

My father and I took my uncle, who recently lost his wife to cancer, fishing. I wanted him to have a good time because he was still shaken up and sad about the loss of my aunt. So I prayed.

I prayed for him to catch fish and get his mind off of his loss for a moment. When I looked up I saw a rainbow in the clouds and remembered that God used the rainbow as a promise once and so I felt like he was promising me that he would answer my prayer. At the end of the day my uncle reeled in 2 groupers, a keeper, and plenty of other fish. He was happy and had a lot of fun. I will never forget that day.

Youth B

Although I had many friends in middle school, I felt detached and didn't feel like I had a lot in common with those friends. The whole middle school experience was not for me. I felt awkward. The one place I was confident, my sport, I was rejected and treated unfairly.

I prayed every day that high school would be better, and it was! Now, I am happy to say that God answered my prayer. The drama is not as intense, I have real friends that I can count on, and I am playing on the team as a starter! God heard my prayer and answered my every wish! I am so glad I have Him to rely on in hard times.

Young adult C

"My fiancé was in so much pain, then it went away after one treatment! I mean, that is pretty amazing to me!" – These words are the only thing I got out of my oldest son when I asked him about miracles in his life. Some people have beautiful elaborate stories and some just tell it like it is! Let me elaborate on his story so you can understand.

For a couple of years, my son's girlfriend, currently fiancé, struggled with pain... intense pain, rendering her unable to walk. The diagnosis was RSD and led to infusion treatments. Infusions are much like chemotherapy. You go to an office for four hours, four days in a row, and are hooked up to a machine. After each procedure, she suffered from nausea, vomiting, weakness, hallucinations and short term memory loss.

Through it all, my son prayed that these intense treatments would work and she would be made whole again. To our pleasant surprise, her pain was gone and she would be up and walking in no time!

His prayer was answered and the wedding is on! Praise the Lord!

Youth D

At church camp was the first time I actually saw evidence of God for myself. It had been a rough year and I had been praying at the altar. A lady I did not know came up to me and prayed for me. She knew actual things that were happening in my life, even though she knew nothing of me. She told me God told her to tell me I was to be a light in my home!

A different relationship was formed between me and the Lord that night. He became real to me, not just a God that my parents talked about.

Youth E

When taking care of a neighbor's dog, I heard from God. The dog refused to come and get the food I set out for her. I knew the food was good for her and without it she would be sick. It was then I realized that God was teaching me a lesson through the dog. God knew what was best for my life and what was good for me. He just wanted me to come to Him and ask and be grateful. I get that now!

Question: Have you ever heard a young child or youth say something about God that struck you as awesome or inspiring? What did they say?

Dig deep: You can make a difference. Think of what you can say to a child or young person and write it in the following area so when the opportunity arises or you make the opportunity you are ready. (i.e. your story, a story from the bible, your miracle, etc.)

Action: Take time this week to talk to a child about where God is present in their life.

Parting Word

We have enjoyed this time with you! These writings are some of the questions, comments, and verses that have been placed on our hearts. Always remember that you are an important person to God and to many others. As you go into the future, we join with the Holy Spirit in prayer that you have a better understanding of who you are in Christ and many blessings come your way!

Love in Him,
Lynn and Christine

Answer Guide/Scriptures

Chapter 1

- "The chords of death entangled me; the torrents of destruction overwhelmed me. The chords of the grave coiled around me; the snares of death confronted me." (Psalm 18:4-5)
- Psalm 18: 6 fill in the blanks: distress, called, cried, help, heard my voice, ears.
- "You were shown these things so that you might know that the Lord is God; besides him there is no other." (Deuteronomy 4:35)

Q: The Lord is God and there is no other

- "Know therefore that the Lord your God is God; he is the faithful God, keeping his covenant of love to a thousand generations of those who love him and keep his commandments." (Deuteronomy 7:9)

Q: He is faithful and keeps his covenant of love for those who love him.

- "Remember your word to your servant, for you have given me hope. My comfort and my suffering is this: your promise preserves my life. The arrogant mock me unmercifully, but I do not turn from your law. I remember, Lord, your ancient laws, and I find comfort in them. (Psalm 119:49-52)
- James 1:20 fill in the blanks: anger, righteousness.
- "In your anger do not sin: do not let the sun go down while you are still angry." (Ephesians 4:26)

Q: Do not sin in your anger.

Chapter 2

- 1Thessalonians 1:4-6 fill in the blanks: chosen you, words, power, Holy Spirit, severe suffering, joy given by the Holy Spirit.

Chapter 3

- "When they came to the other disciples, they saw a large crowd around them and the teachers of the law arguing with them. As soon as all the people saw Jesus, they were overwhelmed with wonder and ran to greet him. "What are you arguing with them about?" he asked. A man in the crowd answered, "Teacher, I brought you my son, who is possessed by a spirit that has robbed him of speech. Whenever it seizes him, it throws him to the ground. He foams at the mouth, gnashes his teeth and becomes rigid. I asked your disciples to drive out the spirit, but they could not." "You unbelieving generation," Jesus replied, "how long shall I stay with you? How long shall I put up with you? Bring the boy to me." So they brought him. When the spirit saw Jesus, it immediately threw the boy into a convulsion. He fell to the ground and rolled around, foaming at the mouth. Jesus asked the boy's father, "How long has he been like this?" "From childhood," he answered. "It has often thrown him into fire or water to kill him. But if you can do anything, take pity on us and help us." "'If you can'?" said Jesus. "Everything is possible for one who believes." Immediately the boy's father exclaimed, "I do believe; help me overcome my unbelief!" When Jesus saw that a crowd was running to the scene, he rebuked the impure spirit. "You deaf and mute spirit," he said, "I command you, come out of him and never enter him again." The spirit shrieked, convulsed him violently and came out. The boy looked so much like a corpse that many said, "He's dead." 27 But Jesus took him by the hand and lifted him to his feet, and he stood up. After Jesus had gone indoors, his disciples asked him privately, "Why couldn't we drive it out?" He replied, "This kind can come out only by prayer." (Mark 9:14-29)
- Proverbs 3:5-6 fill in the blanks: Trust, lean not on your own understanding, paths straight.

Chapter 4

- Six weapons: Word, Prayer, Holy Spirit, Faith, Hope, God's Love
- Ephesians 6:10-18
  New International Version (NIV)
  The Armor of God
  "Finally, be strong in the Lord and in his mighty power. Put on the full armor of God, so that you can take your stand against the devil's schemes. For our struggle is not against flesh and blood, but against the rulers, against the authorities, against the powers of this dark world and against the spiritual forces of evil in the heavenly realms. Therefore put on the full armor of God, so that when the day of evil comes, you may be able to stand your ground, and after you have done everything, to stand. Stand firm then, with the belt of truth buckled around your waist, with the breastplate of righteousness in place, and with your feet fitted with the readiness that comes from the gospel of peace. In addition to all this, take up the shield of faith, with which you can extinguish all the flaming arrows of the evil one. Take the helmet of salvation and the sword of the Spirit, which is the word of God. And pray in the Spirit on all occasions with all kinds of prayers and requests. With this in mind, be alert and always keep on praying for all the Lord's people."

Chapter 5

- Genesis 13:2-18New International Version (NIV)
  Abram had become very wealthy in livestock and in silver and gold. From the Negev he went from place to place until he came to Bethel, to the place between Bethel and Ai where his tent had been earlier ⁴ and where he had first built an altar. There Abram called on the name of the Lord. Now Lot, who was moving about with Abram, also had flocks and herds and tents. But the land could not support them while they stayed together, for their possessions were so great that they were not able to stay together. And quarreling arose between Abram's herders and Lot's. The Canaanites and Perizzites were also living in

the land at that time. So Abram said to Lot, "Let's not have any quarreling between you and me, or between your herders and mine, for we are close relatives. Is not the whole land before you? Let's part company. If you go to the left, I'll go to the right; if you go to the right, I'll go to the left." Lot looked around and saw that the whole plain of the Jordan toward Zoar was well watered, like the garden of the LORD, like the land of Egypt. (This was before the LORD destroyed Sodom and Gomorrah.) So Lot chose for himself the whole plain of the Jordan and set out toward the east. The two men parted company: Abram lived in the land of Canaan, while Lot lived among the cities of the plain and pitched his tents near Sodom. Now the people of Sodom were wicked and were sinning greatly against the LORD. The LORD said to Abram after Lot had parted from him, "Look around from where you are, to the north and south, to the east and west. All the land that you see I will give to you and your offspring forever. I will make your offspring like the dust of the earth, so that if anyone could count the dust, then your offspring could be counted. Go, walk through the length and breadth of the land, for I am giving it to you." So Abram went to live near the great trees of Mamre at Hebron, where he pitched his tents. There he built an altar to the LORD.

Chapter 6
Q: promise: the peace of God.
Q: "tool": praise

Chapter 8
- Ecclesiastes 7:13-14 fill in the blanks: good, happy, bad, consider, anything, future.

Q: No one can discover anything about their future.
- "My eyes will be on the faithful and the land. That they may dwell with me; the one who's walk is blameless will minister to me. (Psalm 101:6)

Chapter 9

- Four commands: choose life, love the Lord your God, listen to His voice, hold fast to Him.

Chapter 10

- Psalm 37:7-9 fill in the blanks: still, wait patiently, fret not, refrain, forsake, Fret not, wait, shall.

Q: wait, fret

Chapter 11

- 2 Corinthians 4:16-17: heart, outwardly, inwardly, momentary troubles, outweighs.

Chapter 14

- "If we claim to be without sin, we deceive ourselves and the truth is not in us. If we confess our sins, he is faithful and just and will forgive us our sins and purify us from all unrighteousness. If we claim we have not sinned, we make him out to be a liar and his word is not in us." (1 John 1:8-10)
- James 5:16 fill in the blank: confess your sins, you may be healed, righteous.

Chapter 15

- 30 times

Chapter 17

- 2 Corinthians 2:10-11 fill in the blanks: Anyone, I also forgive, Satan, his schemes.

Chapter 19

- Matthew 17:14-20 fill in the blanks: have mercy, disciples, could not, how long, how long, at that moment, why couldn't we drive it out, so little faith, faith.
- "Consequently, faith comes from hearing the message, and the message is heard through the word about Christ." (Romans 10:17)

Works Cited

Control._(n.d.). *Online etymology dictionary.* Retrieved April 24, 2014 from dictionary.com website: http://dictionary.reference.com/browse/trust

Lynn & Christine (2013). God's Promises (p.60). In *The Rose Garden and the Ring.* Bloomington, ID: WestBow Press.

Submit._(n.d.). *Online etymology dictionary.* Retrieved April 24, 2014 from dictionary.com website: http://dictionary.reference.com/browse/trust

Trust. (n.d.). *Online etymology dictionary.* Retrieved April 24, 2014 from dictionary.com website: http://dictionary.reference.com/browse/trust

The Zondervan Corporation. (2014-2015). Multiple NIV verses. Retrieved in 2014-2015 from www.biblegateway.com

About the Authors

Lynn---Wife, Mother, Domestic Goddess, Military Veteran, Property Manager, Student and most importantly Christian. Lynn's faith has been tested time and time again but nothing has compared to surviving the affair of a spouse. No doubt the effects of adultery no one should have to endure but with God you can come through not only a better person but stronger in faith and living a more fulfilled life! She hopes to, through this study guide, help more people get through or at least have a better understanding of any crises they are going through. Lynn continues to live, work, and grow in Christ with her two children and golden retriever.

Christine---Wife, Mother, Domestic Goddess, Vocalist, Seamstress, Baker, and most importantly Christian. Christine has endured the ravaging effects of her spouse's betrayal. This life altering experience should never be a part of a person's testimony but is rampant in today's culture. While unfortunate she is able to use her testimony for God's glory. Christine, her husband, and four children reside, work, and grow in Christ.

Check it out...

The Rose Garden
And the Ring
Faith in the Midst of Unfaithfulness
By: Lynn and Christine

In *The Rose Garden and the Ring*, you will discover that you are not alone. The tools and insight gained from the pages of this labor of love can bring comfort in the emotional moments to persevere with God.

This heartfelt and honest account of two ordinary yet very different women goes beyond just saying life will get better with Christ and delves into the actual process one goes through on the road to healing from a spouse's affair.

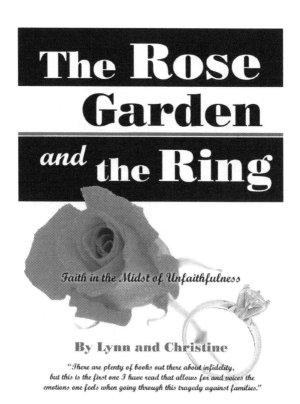

The Rose
Garden
and the Ring

Faith in the Midst of Unfaithfulness

By Lynn and Christine

"There are plenty of books out there about infidelity, but this is the first one I have read that allows for and voices the emotions one feels when going through this tragedy against families."

We invite you to grow spiritually and heal your heart with the **Faith in the Midst Study Guide**; a companion to the original book, **The Rose Garden and the Ring**.

Keep Connected...

Feel free to contact us through our Facebook page:
https://www.facebook.com/pages/The-Rose-Garden-and-the-Ring/519131274831633?fref=ts

Printed in the United States
By Bookmasters